MEGA-COOL
MEGAFAUNA
Creatures of Today
Anastasia Suen

A Division of

Carson
Dellosa
Education

ROURKE'S
SCHOOL to HOME
CONNECTIONS
BEFORE AND DURING READING ACTIVITIES

Before Reading: *Building Background Knowledge and Vocabulary*

Building background knowledge can help children process new information and build upon what they already know. Before reading a book, it is important to tap into what children already know about the topic. This will help them develop their vocabulary and increase their reading comprehension.

Questions and Activities to Build Background Knowledge:

1. Look at the front cover of the book and read the title. What do you think this book will be about?
2. What do you already know about this topic?
3. Take a book walk and skim the pages. Look at the table of contents, photographs, captions, and bold words. Did these text features give you any information or predictions about what you will read in this book?

Vocabulary: *Vocabulary Is Key to Reading Comprehension*

Use the following directions to prompt a conversation about each word.

- Read the vocabulary words.
- What comes to mind when you see each word?
- What do you think each word means?

Vocabulary Words:

- average
- baleen
- carnivore
- crustaceans
- echolocation
- equator
- herbivore
- hibernation
- megafauna
- omnivore

During Reading: *Reading for Meaning and Understanding*

To achieve deep comprehension of a book, children are encouraged to use close reading strategies. During reading, it is important to have children stop and make connections. These connections result in deeper analysis and understanding of a book.

 Close Reading a Text

During reading, have children stop and talk about the following:

- Any confusing parts
- Any unknown words
- Text to text, text to self, text to world connections
- The main idea in each chapter or heading

Encourage children to use context clues to determine the meaning of any unknown words. These strategies will help children learn to analyze the text more thoroughly as they read.

When you are finished reading this book, turn to the next-to-last page for **Text-Dependent Questions** and an **Extension Activity**.

Table of Contents

Today's Mega Creatures

Scientists say that 299 million to 273 million years ago, Earth only had one continent. All around this continent, named Pangaea, was an ocean called Panthalassa.

As time passed, the land moved and new continents formed. Today, there are seven continents and five oceans. Each has very large animals. **Megafauna** live on the land, in the sky, and in the sea.

How do some animals grow so large? They must eat a lot of food to be able to reach mega-sized status. An animal that only eat plants is an **herbivore**. An animal that only eats other animals is a **carnivore**. An animal that eats both is an **omnivore**.

Pangaea

- Asia
- Europe
- North America
- Africa
- South America
- Antarctica
- Australia
- Panthalassa

From One Ocean to Five

The Pacific Ocean, the Atlantic Ocean, the Arctic Ocean, and the Indian Ocean are the oldest named oceans. In 2000, the Southern Ocean (circling Antarctica) was named by the International Hydrographic Organization.

The World Today

- Arctic Ocean
- North America
- Europe
- Asia
- Atlantic Ocean
- Africa
- South America
- Pacific Ocean
- Indian Ocean
- Australia
- Southern Ocean
- Antarctica

Herbivores Today

African elephants are enormous herbivores that can weigh up to 14,000 pounds (6,350 kilograms) and grow up to 13 feet (four meters) tall. To grow that big, they need to eat a lot! African elephants eat four to seven percent of their body weight in grasses, herbs, fruit, plants and trees each day. They can consume up to 600 pounds (272 kilograms) of food a day!

In and Out

African elephants don't digest all of the food they eat. These gentle giants produce up to 330 pounds (150 kilograms) of dung per day. Then other animals, such as dung beetles, eat it.

Which megafauna eat fruit at night and sleep all day? It's the giant golden-crowned flying fox found in the Philippines. These megabats can have a wingspan of 5.5 feet (about 1.6 meters). However, they weigh less than three pounds (one kilogram).

During the day, these megabats roost together upside down in the treetops. They wrap their long wings around themselves and hang from their claws. At night, they eat figs, their favorite food. They also chew on the leaves of fig trees.

Night Vision

*Unlike other bats that use **echolocation** to find their way, these megabats use their sight and sense of smell to find food at night. A megabat pup clings to its mother's fur as she flies.*

Dugongs are the only herbivorous mammals in the sea. (A mammal is a warm-blooded animal with a backbone. Mammals have hair or fur and make milk.) Like all mammals, dugongs breathe air. After six minutes underwater, a dugong comes up to breathe. It can stand on its tail and put its head above the water.

Dugongs live along the coast in the sea grass beds of the Indian and Pacific Oceans. They grow to 13 feet (four meters) long as they eat the sea grass along eastern Africa and Australia. A dugong can weigh up to 595 pounds (270 kilograms).

Carnivores Today

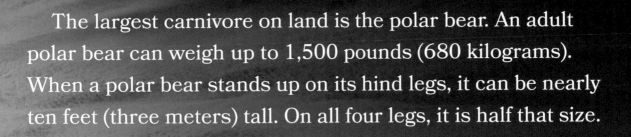

The largest carnivore on land is the polar bear. An adult polar bear can weigh up to 1,500 pounds (680 kilograms). When a polar bear stands up on its hind legs, it can be nearly ten feet (three meters) tall. On all four legs, it is half that size.

Polar bears eat seals. When a polar bear finds a seal's breathing hole in the ice, it can smell the seal. The polar bear waits for the seal to come up for air. When the ice melts, polar bears can't find seals, so they have nothing to eat.

At 12 feet (about 3.6 meters) across, the wandering albatross has the largest wingspan of any bird. It flies over the southern oceans looking for fish and squid near the surface of the water. Wandering albatrosses can glide over the water for hours without flapping their wings. When they're not looking for food, these 28-pound (12.7-kilogram) birds sleep on the surface of the water itself. The wandering albatross only visits land when it is breeding.

The biggest carnivore in the sea eats one of the smallest creatures. The blue whale grows to 90 feet (27 meters) long by eating tiny krill. When a blue whale opens its mouth, it captures thousands of tiny krill all at once. Then, the blue whale closes its mouth and uses its tongue to push the water out through its **baleen** plates. All that food is how a blue whale can grow to 300,000 pounds (136,078 kilograms).

Blue whales are larger than some boats.

Seen from Space

*Krill are small **crustaceans** that look like shrimp. Their **average** size is two inches (five centimeters), about the length of a paper clip. They live in enormous swarms that can be seen from outer space!*

Omnivores Today

The 1,500-pound (680-kilogram) Kodiak bear is the largest land omnivore in the modern world. It only lives on Kodiak Island off the coast of Alaska. When it stands on its hind legs, a Kodiak bear can be roughly ten feet (about three meters) tall. On all four legs, it is five feet (1.5 meters) tall. After **hibernation**, Kodiak bears travel down the mountain to look for food below the snowline. They eat grass, roots, berries, and fish. They also eat dead seals, deer, and other carrion that they find.

The heaviest animal to fly is the 42-pound (19-kilogram) kori bustard. Their wingspan can be up to nine feet (2.7 meters). In the grasslands, scrublands, and savannahs of Africa, these birds eat insects, reptiles, small mammals, and even other birds. They also eat seeds, berries, and the gum of the Acacia tree. In the Afrikaans language, a kori bustard is called a *gompou*, which means "gum-eating bird."

Watch Out!
Ostriches are also birds, but they don't fly. They grow large by eating roots, seeds, leaves, lizards, locusts, rodents, and snakes. If you bother one, this 320-pound (145-kilogram) bird will kick and bite you!

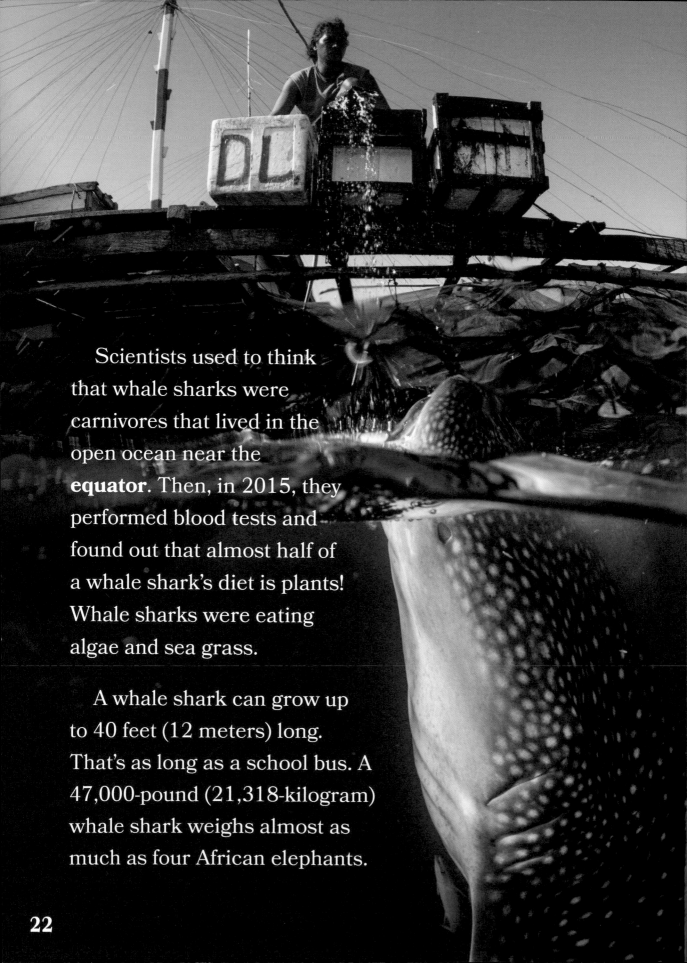

Scientists used to think
that whale sharks were
carnivores that lived in the
open ocean near the
equator. Then, in 2015, they
performed blood tests and
found out that almost half of
a whale shark's diet is plants!
Whale sharks were eating
algae and sea grass.

A whale shark can grow up
to 40 feet (12 meters) long.
That's as long as a school bus. A
47,000-pound (21,318-kilogram)
whale shark weighs almost as
much as four African elephants.

Eating Krill like Whales

Whale sharks eat krill that they trap with baleen at the back of their throats. They also eat fish eggs, squid, prawns, and small fish. Unlike blue whales, when a whale shark swallows water, it doesn't push it out through its mouth. Instead, it pushes the water through its gills.

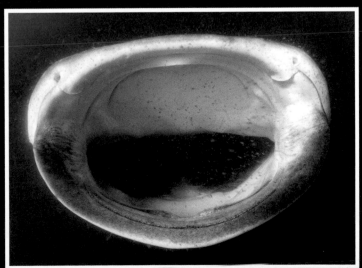

What Is the Largest?

What is the largest animal on land? The answer depends on what you are measuring. Depending on what you are comparing, such as height or weight, different animals could be considered the largest. For example, an African elephant is taller than a Kodiak or a polar bear and could be called the largest animal in the group.

Land Animal Height on All Four Legs

Measurements in meters

1. **African elephant**: 13 feet (4 meters) tall
2. **polar bear**: 5 feet (1.5 meters) tall
3. **Kodiak bear**: 5 feet (1.5 meters) tall

You can also compare animal weights. The African elephant is also heavier than both bears. It could be considered the largest animal in the group based on weight as well.

Holding the Record

African elephants are not the tallest animals on Earth. That title belongs to the giraffe. This herbivore can grow up to around 18 feet (5.5 meters) tall and uses its height to reach leaves on tall trees.

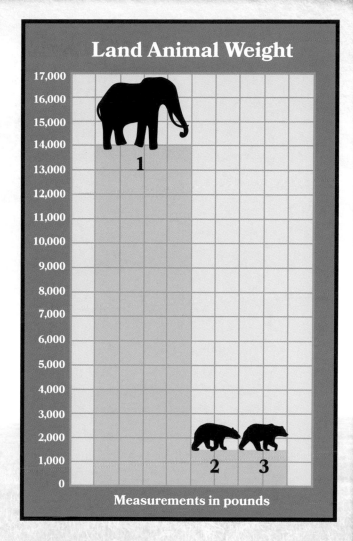

Land Animal Weight

17,000
16,000
15,000
14,000
13,000
12,000
11,000
10,000
9,000
8,000
7,000
6,000
5,000
4,000
3,000
2,000
1,000
0

1

2   3

Measurements in pounds

1. **African elephant**: 14,000 pounds (6,350 kilograms)
2. **polar bear**: 1,500 pounds (680 kilograms)
3. **Kodiak bear**: 1,500 pounds (680 kilograms)

What is the largest animal in the sky? Wingspan is one way to measure that. When you compare the wingspans of flying animals, the wandering albatross is the largest.

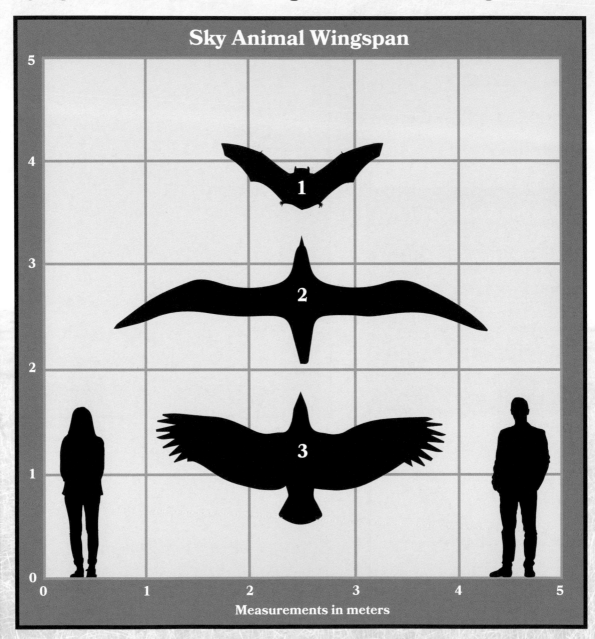

1. **giant golden-crowned flying fox**: 5.5 feet (1.6 meters)
2. **wandering albatross**: 12 feet (3.6 meters)
3. **kori bustard**: nine feet (2.7 meters)

You can compare weight as well. Among these modern flying megafauna, the kori bustard weighs the most.

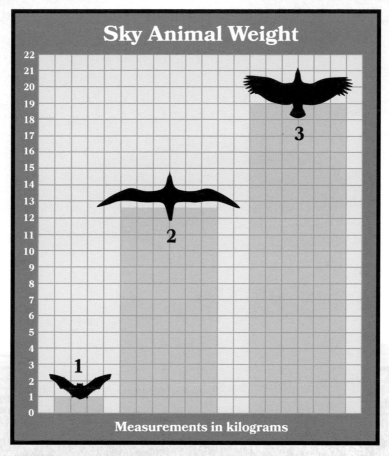

Sky Animal Weight

Measurements in kilograms

1. **giant golden-crowned flying fox**: less than three pounds (one kilogram)
2. **wandering albatross**: 28 pounds (12.7 kilograms)
3. **kori bustard**: 42 pounds (19 kilograms)

Eating, Not Flying

Kori bustards are the heaviest flying animals, but they spend most of their time walking around looking for food. They are much lighter than the ostrich, however, which is also a bird but it does not fly at all.

Animals in the water can be measured the same way. One way to measure the largest one is by length.

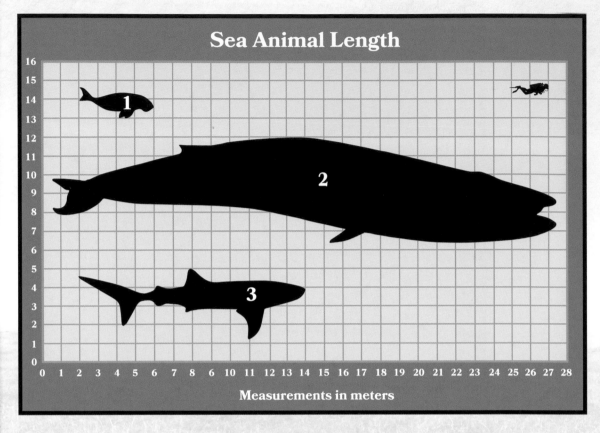

Sea Animal Length

Measurements in meters

1. **dugong**: 13 feet (four meters) long
2. **blue whale**: 90 feet (27 meters) long
3. **whale shark**: 40 feet (12 meters) long

A Champion Eater

A whale shark weighs as much as four African elephants. However, it is smaller than a blue whale that will eat 12,000 pounds (5,443 kilograms) of krill a day during feeding season.

The blue whale is the longest animal in the sea. That is why some people consider it the largest. Sea animals can also be compared by weight. The blue whale is the largest animal by weight as well.

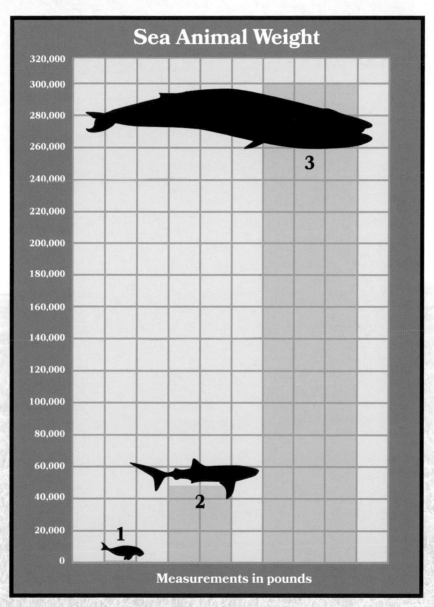

Sea Animal Weight

Measurements in pounds

1. **dugong**: 595 pounds (270 kilograms)
2. **blue whale**: 300,000 pounds (136,078 kilograms)
3. **whale shark**: 47,000 pounds (21,318 kilograms)

Glossary

average (AV-uh-rij): usual or ordinary

baleen (buh-LEEN): an elastic, rough substance that forms thin plates in the upper jaw of some whales

carnivore (KAHR-nuh-vawr): an animal that only eats other animals

crustaceans (kruh-STEY-shuh-ns): aquatic arthropods with a hard shell or crust, including lobsters, shrimps, crabs, and barnacles

echolocation (ek-oh-loh-KAY-shuhn): the location of items by listening for a sound to echo back from them

equator (ih-KWAY-tur): an imaginary line around the middle of the Earth halfway between the North and South Poles

herbivore (HUR-buh-vawr): an animal that eats only plants

hibernation (HYE-bur-nay-shuhn): an inactive state that looks like deep sleep that animals enter in cold winter climates

megafauna (MEG-uh-faw-nuh): giant animals

omnivore (OM-nuh-vawr): an animal that eats both plants and other animals

Index

Text-Dependent Questions

1. Why can more than one animal be considered the largest?

2. How does a polar bear find seals to eat?

3. What happens if you attack an ostrich?

4. How did scientists find out that whale sharks were omnivores?

5. Why could an African elephant be considered the largest modern land animal?

Extension Activity

Create an infographic that compares two modern megafauna living on Earth today. Include their location, diet, and three other items such as weight or height. Decide which is the largest and explain your answer.

About the Author

Anastasia Suen is the author of more than 350 books for children, teens, and adults. She lives near the sea in Northern California, where blue whales swim as they migrate each year.

© 2021 Rourke Educational Media

www.rourkeeducationalmedia.com

PHOTO CREDITS: cover: Shutterstock / GettyImages / slowmotiongli; pages 3-9: Shutterstock; page 9: GettyImages/ nikkigensert; pages 10-11: Shutterstock / © LauraDin; pages 12-13: Shutterstock; pages 14-15: GettyImages / Manakin / burroblando; pages 16-17: GettyImages / © eco2drew; page 17: (inset) GettyImages / Allexxandar / (inset) ©NASA's Earth Observatory; page 18: Shutterstock; page 19: GettyImages / slowmotiongli; pages 20-21: Shutterstock; pages 22: Danita Delimont Photography / Newscom; pages 23: Shutterstock; page 25: (inset) Shutterstock; page 27: (inset) Shutterstock; page 29: (inset) GettyImages / © MR1805

Edited by: Tracie Santos
Cover and interior design by: Lynne Schwaner

Library of Congress PCN Data

Creatures of Today / Anastasia Suen
(Mega-Cool Megafauna)
ISBN 978-1-73164-351-3 (hard cover)(alk. paper)
ISBN 978-1-73164-315-5 (soft cover)
ISBN 978-1-73164-383-4 (e-Book)
ISBN 978-1-73164-415-2 (ePub)
Library of Congress Control Number: 2020945102

Rourke Educational Media
Printed in the United States of America
01-3502011937